THE TRILATERAL FORCE:
THE ATLANTIC ALLIANCE AND THE FUTURE OF NUCLEAR WEAPONS

STRATEGY

INTRODUCTION

During a now famous speech in Prague in 2009, President Obama emphasized twenty-first century nuclear dangers, declaring that to overcome these threats, the United States will "seek the peace and security of a world without nuclear weapons."[1] Foreign policy analysts viewed President Obama's statement as a reaffirmed commitment by the United States to eventual nuclear disarmament. In historical context, President Obama articulated what is clearly a disarmament trajectory that began in the 1960s and only accelerated with the collapse of the Soviet Union. Since the end of the Cold War, the United States and Russia together reduced operationally deployed strategic nuclear weapons by seventy-five percent, though much work remains to be done as both nations still retain substantially more nuclear weapons than they need for deterrence.[2]

Under the New Strategic Arms Reduction Treaty, the United States and Russia agreed to the following mutual limits by 2018:[3]

- 1,550 accountable deployed strategic warheads
- 700 deployed intercontinental ballistic missiles, deployed submarine-launched ballistic missiles, and deployed nuclear-capable heavy bombers
- A combined limit of 800 deployed and non-deployed strategic launchers

This is certainly progress toward the goal of eliminating nuclear weapons. In the four years since President Obama's 2009 Prague speech, however, the nuclear predicament has become more complex and

---

* The views expressed in this article are those of the author and do not necessarily reflect the official policy or position of the United States Air Force, Department of Defense, or United States Government.

more precarious with little sign of movement toward abolition. Nuclear war between major nuclear armed states is unlikely. On the other hand, nuclear terrorism and nuclear proliferation, particularly the Iranian and North Korean nuclear weapons programs which could trigger chains of proliferation, are the urgent nuclear priorities that could lead to regional nuclear weapons use.[4] In fact, as Bracken argues, during the Cold War, nuclear weapons arose out of the existential need for survival and the concomitant requirement to be able to utterly destroy an ideological adversary. In the current age, nuclear weapons emerge from the normal dynamics of insecurity and regional balance of power politics. Consequently, there is now no overarching conceptual framework such as deterrence or containment that can adequately deal with the variations of strategic personality of every individual country. The concepts of deterrence and containment may be limited to the Cold War and their application may not impact the world of today.[5]

Countervailing nuclear realities have overcome the idea of global zero. Walker nicely describes the tension between the Obama Administration's desire for the elimination of nuclear weapons and doubts leading to restraint in pursuing that goal.[6] The fundamental flaw in the concept of global zero is not its desirability, but its enforceability. Lieber and Press also make a strong case that changes in military technology and the balance of power call into question the desirability, as well, of further nuclear reductions.[7]

During a speech in Berlin in 2013, President Obama attempted to reinvigorate the nuclear arms reduction process while recognizing the limits of such efforts due to current geopolitical nuclear realties. He called for reducing the number of United States strategic warheads by one-third, as well as a substantial cut in the number of deployed tactical nuclear warheads, if the Russian government agrees to a similar cut.[8] Follow-on nuclear employment strategic guidance confirmed a one-third reduction in deployed nuclear weapons from the level established in the New Strategic Arms Reduction Treaty.[9]

The United States seems trapped in the policy paradox of desiring continued nuclear arms reductions while recognizing the current reality of needing to maintain a robust nuclear arms deterrent. Therefore, how can the United States balance these two imperatives?

- The desire to work toward a world free of nuclear weapons
- The need to retain nuclear weapons to deter attack on the United States and its allies while nuclear weapons still exist

More specifically and operationally, how far can the United States decrease its nuclear weapons stockpile and still maintain the required effective deterrent? How many nuclear weapons are enough?

The concept of strategic stability is instructive here.[10] Strategic stability is a central characteristic of a relationship in which neither side could gain a positive outcome from the employment of its nuclear weapons, and it therefore would have no incentive for nuclear threats or attacks. This is both a quantitative and a qualitative construct within strategic relationships. Ultimately though, the credibility of the United States nuclear umbrella lies in the guarantee of the United States and not on the specific number or location of its nuclear weapons. Thus, how low can the United States take its nuclear arsenal in pursuit of arms reduction goals and still preserve strategic stability among the world's nuclear powers, while maintaining a credible minimal deterrence posture?

United States officials are looking at a cut that would take the nuclear arsenal of deployed weapons to between 1,000 and 900, and perhaps even as low as 700, with only half deployed.[11] President Obama, during his Berlin speech, proposed a reduction to slightly over 1,000.[12] The current fiscal crisis in the United States is also instructive. As future budgetary limitations target Department of Defense reductions, the United States may further reduce its nuclear weapons posture in the name of fiscal responsibility. If the number of United States nuclear weapons eventually drops to the level of its allies, the United Kingdom and France, around 200-300 deployed weapons, can the United States still meet its security commitments and maintain a credible extended deterrent? Perhaps the United States cannot do so alone. In fact, the possibility and desirability of nuclear coalition operations has been frequently raised, but not developed, in discussions on the nuclear weapons drawdown and continuing deterrence and extended deterrence requirements with senior members of the United States nuclear policy community since 2009.[13]

Any reductions must not undercut strategic stability with established nuclear powers. Strategic stability requires that all nuclear weapons states commit to the same definition of minimal credible deterrence. Thus, any future multilateral arms reductions must link the floor of United States and Russian reductions with ceiling commitments for the nuclear arsenals of China, the United Kingdom, France, India, and Pakistan.[14] Only once the world's nuclear powers reach global parity can they then seriously begin the work of further reductions to reach global zero.

This paper explores the operational ramifications of eventually reaching this level of nuclear parity by examining how the United States can meet its security commitments, maintaining a credible extended deterrence, while reducing its nuclear arsenal to the minimum level required, achieving and maintaining strategic stability among the world's nuclear powers. I begin by examining both the quantitative and qualitative implications of future nuclear arms reductions by the United States, determining that, in the future, only through nuclear coalition operations can the United States continue to meet its national security commitments at minimum deterrence levels.

I then shift to examining the strategic feasibility of nuclear coalition operations. I explore the grand strategies, security strategies, and nuclear weapons strategies of the United States, the United Kingdom, France, the North Atlantic Treaty Organization, and the European Union to ascertain if and where synergies exist in the nuclear weapons policies of these security community allies. This analysis suggests that cooperation between the United States, the United Kingdom, and France on the strategic, operational, and tactical levels is theoretically a viable means of maintaining a Nuclear Triad capable of meeting extended deterrence security commitments, while preserving strategic stability at the lowest possible nuclear arsenal levels.

Next, I examine the operational and tactical feasibility of nuclear coalition operations. A future Atlantic Alliance trilateral nuclear force structure between the United States, the United Kingdom, and France is a possible means to achieve shared national security objectives. This paper concludes by proposing several possible options for the configuration of a Trilateral Force and argues that the best option is a phased approach linking current and future force structure needs with arms reduction goals instead of considering the two issues in isolation. Finally, while nuclear coalition cooperation at the strategic level is not only viable, but essential among the three allies, operationalizing a trilateral force structure may prove extremely difficult without a shared existential threat perception, among other challenges.

HOW LOW CAN YOU GO?

Any discussion of the ramifications of nuclear weapons reductions must begin with the reductions themselves. Clearly, the United States is on a steep trajectory of reductions from a high in 1966 of 32,000 nuclear warheads[15] to an estimated 7,650 warheads today.[16] New Strategic Arms Reduction Treaty reductions will bring the total of deployed nuclear warheads down to 1,550[17] with further reductions considered to between 900-1,000 and perhaps as low as 700,[18] although the current proposal is slightly over 1,000.[19] As of March 1, 2013, the United States arsenal of strategic offensive arms consists of:[20]

- 792 deployed intercontinental ballistic missiles, deployed submarine-launched ballistic missiles, and deployed nuclear-capable heavy bombers
- 1,654 warheads on deployed intercontinental ballistic missiles, on deployed submarine-launched ballistic missiles, and nuclear warheads counted for deployed nuclear-capable heavy bombers
- 1,028 deployed and non-deployed launchers of intercontinental ballistic missiles, deployed and non-deployed launchers of submarine-launched ballistic missiles, and deployed and non-deployed nuclear-capable heavy bombers

If this trajectory holds into the future, nuclear arms reductions by the United States will at some point reach parity with its allies, the United Kingdom and France, at 225-300 nuclear warheads.[21] Can the United States still meet its security commitments and maintain a credible extended deterrence at these levels? Several researchers explore this issue and some offer low end estimates of acceptable United States nuclear arsenal levels to meet these goals.

Blair and colleagues examined several variables of United States and Russian force structure, alert posture, accuracy, yields, etc., via computer simulations to reach the conclusion that both countries could limit their strategic nuclear arsenals to 1,000 warheads with no more than 500 launchers without weakening security.[22] Deutch suggests the following force structure of less than 1,000 warheads: nine

Trident submarines each with 16 missiles with eight nuclear warheads each, with three at sea at a time constituting 384 warheads on alert; with another 200 supplemental intercontinental ballistic missiles and air platform warheads for flexibility.[23] Forsyth and colleagues propose a minimum deterrence strategy of 311 warheads dispersed on 100 single warhead intercontinental ballistic missiles, 192 warheads on 12 submarines each carrying 24 missiles, and 19 B-2s.[24] Cimbala argues that a minimum deterrence regime at either 1,000 or 500 deployed strategic nuclear weapons could provide both Russia and the United States nuclear security and stability.[25] Finally, Global Zero argues for 900 total strategic weapons by 2022 with only 450 on alert.[26]

These scholars all agree that the United States could still meet its security commitments and maintain credible extended deterrence with a nuclear arsenal somewhere between 300-1,000 warheads, a potential reduction as high as ninety-two percent from current levels and as high as a sixty-one percent reduction from agreed upon New Strategic Arms Reduction Treaty levels. When reductions begin to approach these levels, the operational ramifications become more pronounced. Can the United States still effectively maintain the Nuclear Triad at these lower levels? Several researchers explore this issue and offer recommendations.

Johnson and colleagues looked at all of the various postures among the current Nuclear Triad and concluded that submarine-launched ballistic missiles and intercontinental ballistic missiles provide clear advantages over other options, forming a future Nuclear Dyad, and that the United States should phase the bomber force out of the nuclear mission.[27] On the other hand, Lowther makes some convincing arguments in favor of maintaining all three legs of the Nuclear Triad.[28] Lieber and Press note that China maintains effective deterrence with 18 intercontinental ballistic missiles, with four warheads each, and 60 short-range nuclear missiles, though China is also developing mobile intercontinental ballistic missiles and submarine-launched ballistic missiles.[29] On the other hand, they also note that the increased accuracy and lethality of Trident submarine missiles, increased guidance accuracy of intercontinental ballistic missiles, and improved radar avoidance avionics on the B-2 all suggest that the United States could maintain the Nuclear Triad at lower numbers of overall warheads.[30] They advocate that the United States must preserve this mix of capabilities as it cuts the size of its nuclear force. The United States needs some high-yield nuclear weapons, although fewer than it currently possesses, and must retain the lowest-yield warheads while enhancing their accuracy.[31] Reif and colleagues discuss the pros and cons of each leg of the Nuclear Triad and conclude that a policy of minimum deterrence will require reductions to all three legs of the Nuclear Triad, but the United States should preserve each leg with the submarine force as the centerpiece of deterrence policy.[32]

In a comprehensive study that examined the qualitative implications of a reduced nuclear arsenal, Larsen and colleagues came to several important conclusions. A reduced nuclear arsenal must meet three specific force requirements:

- Deterring and prevailing over peer adversaries requires survivability and the ability to defeat defenses to ensure a devastating response to an adversary's first strike
- Deterring and prevailing over a regional actor with a small nuclear arsenal requires accuracy, promptness, and a variety of yield options
- Assuring allies requires a nuclear force with an ability to signal intent to ensure the efficacy of nuclear umbrellas

The key qualitative characteristics of today's nuclear force structure remain critical to tomorrow's smaller nuclear force structure as well.[33]

We can draw several conclusions from this discussion regarding the ramifications of nuclear weapons reductions:

- The United States commits to eventual further reductions, perhaps below 1,000 nuclear warheads
- This drawdown trajectory, coupled with current and future fiscal constraints, suggests that it is inevitable that the United States will institute further reductions, eventually taking its nuclear arsenal below 500 warheads, although with serious sustainment questions
- The United States commits to maintaining the Nuclear Triad, especially the submarine-launched ballistic missile fleet, although reductions to all three legs of the Triad are necessary to achieve overall reduction goals
- To ensure its national security, the United States must maintain the ability to meet all three qualitative force requirements regardless of the quantitative numbers in its nuclear arsenal: Deter peers, deter regional actors, and assure allies

Can a United States nuclear arsenal, reduced to levels of parity with its allies the United Kingdom and France, at 225-300 nuclear warheads, continue to deter and prevail over peer adversaries and regional actors, as well as signal assurance to allies? It is unlikely that the United States will be able to continue to meet these requirements alone. Thus, the United States requires a future nuclear force structure based on nuclear coalition operations.

NUCLEAR COALITION OPERATIONS AT THE STRATEGIC LEVEL

Before offering any potential options on future coalition nuclear force structures, we must explore the strategic feasibility of nuclear coalition operations. For only if the allied nations in question share the same strategies regarding nuclear weapons policies is nuclear coalition operationalization possible. Thus, this section explores the grand strategies, security strategies, and nuclear weapons strategies of the United States, the United Kingdom, France, the North Atlantic Treaty Organization, and the European Union to ascertain if and where synergies exist in the nuclear weapons policies of these security community allies.

DEFINING GRAND STRATEGY

If there is such a thing as a grand strategy, what is it? Theoretically, the broad outlines of the grand strategies of nations are historically clear, even if they were not always clear to the decision makers of any given era. A grand strategy is rarely a declared element of national policy. Rather, it is a set of subconscious guidelines followed by successive governments regardless of ideology. Grand strategies develop in stages, seeking to achieve specific geopolitical imperatives. Pragmatically, a grand strategy is a calculated relation of means to large ends. It is a nation's overarching national goals aligning a range of national resources to meet those goals. It is not just lofty goals, because goals without resources to achieve them are a strategy doomed to failure. It is also not just about mobilizing means, because a strategy is about mobilizing resources to achieve the larger ends of the nation. Grand strategy requires that resources align with goals. If they do not align with goals, or if goals are ill-defined, it is bad strategy.

GRAND, SECURITY, AND NUCLEAR WEAPONS STRATEGIES OF THE UNITED STATES

The grand strategy of the United States is to prevent any potential challengers to American hegemony from rising through engagement. American engagement takes two forms:[34]

- Cooperation (Economic and security interdependence and collaboration)
- Empire (Direct American expeditionary military intervention)

To achieve this goal, the United States first had to meet several historical geopolitical imperatives. A fledgling United States had to dominate the greater Mississippi basin, and eventually all of North America, through expanding colonization, conquest, and concessions. After consolidation, the United States had to eliminate all land-based threats to the greater Mississippi basin. As an ascendant power, the United States had to allow no power to emerge in the Western Hemisphere to challenge the American domination of North America. To ensure this, the United States had to control the ocean approaches to North America, and the waters of the Western Hemisphere, to prevent the approach of any foreign military power. Finally, to secure its place as a global superpower post-World War II, the United States needed to dominate the world's oceans to protect global trade and ensure that no power could build a navy to challenge the United States.[35]

With the fall of the Soviet Union after the Cold War, the United States remained as the only global superpower. To retain this position, the current geopolitical imperative of the United States is to prevent any potential challengers from rising, ensuring that no single continental power arises on the Eurasian landmass capable of challenging the United States. The greatest threat to the current hegemonic position of the United States is America's own tendency to retreat from international events.[36]

How does the security strategy of the United States meet its grand strategy goals? The United States security strategy commits to American leadership coupled with extensive partnerships to shape the international system and meet twenty-first century challenges. Taking a strategic approach to meeting its top national security priorities, the United States strategy focuses on enduring interests. These interests include:

- The security of the United States, its citizens, and United States allies and partners
- A strong, innovative, and growing United States economy in an open international economic system that promotes opportunity and prosperity
- Respect for universal values at home and around the world
- An international order advanced by United States leadership that promotes peace, security, and opportunity through stronger cooperation to meet global challenges

The United States seeks to advance security, prosperity, value, and international order interests.[37]

The United States hopes to shape its vision of the world by pursuing comprehensive engagement and promoting a just and sustainable international order. The United States asserts that military force may at times be necessary to defend America and her allies to preserve peace and security and to protect civilians in the event of a humanitarian crisis. This means credibly guaranteeing United States defense commitments with tailored deterrence capabilities, while helping allies to build similar capacities, to achieve regional and global security. Although the United States commits to exhausting all other options before war, the United States reserves the right to act unilaterally to defend the nation and American interests through the use of force.[38]

How does the nuclear weapons strategy of the United States meet its security strategy goals? The United States focuses on five key objectives for its nuclear weapons policies and posture:[39]

- Preventing nuclear proliferation and nuclear terrorism
- Reducing the role of nuclear weapons in the national security strategy
- Maintaining strategic deterrence and stability at reduced nuclear force levels
- Strengthening regional deterrence and reassuring allies and partners
- Sustaining a safe, secure, and effective nuclear arsenal

In addition, a Department of Defense report to Congress added a sixth objective:[40]

- Achieving objectives if deterrence fails

The United States shapes its nuclear weapons policies and force structure in ways that will better enable meeting the most pressing security challenges. The United States seeks to:[41]

- Reduce the role and numbers of its nuclear weapons
- Maintain a credible nuclear deterrent while reinforcing regional security architectures with missile defenses and other conventional military capabilities
- Pursue a sound Stockpile Management Program for extending the life of its nuclear weapons, modernize its aging nuclear facilities, and invest in human capital
- Promote strategic stability with Russia and China and improve transparency and mutual confidence
- Work to reduce the salience of nuclear weapons in international affairs while moving step-by-step toward eliminating its nuclear weapons

In its attempt to reduce the role of nuclear weapons in its security strategy, the United States makes several specific policy claims with clear ramifications for the future of its nuclear weapons strategy:[42]

- The deterrence of nuclear attack on the United States or its allies and partners is the primary purpose of its nuclear weapons
- The United States would only consider the use of nuclear weapons in extreme circumstances to defend the vital interests of the United States or its allies and partners
- The United States will not use or threaten to use nuclear weapons against non-nuclear weapons states that are party to the Non-Proliferation Treaty and are in compliance with their nuclear nonproliferation obligations
- The United States will maintain a credible nuclear deterrent capable of convincing adversaries that the consequences of attack outweigh the potential benefits gained
- The United States policy is to achieve credible deterrence with the lowest possible number of nuclear weapons

Thus, future United States nuclear strategy will need to focus on:[43]

- The safety of nuclear materials
- Sustaining the credibility of extended deterrence
- Institutionalizing the Comprehensive Nuclear Test Ban Treaty
- Capping global production of fissile material
- Devaluing the role of nuclear weapons in global security

These strategic policy choices have implications for the future nuclear force structure.

The United States currently maintains 7,650 estimated warheads,[44] with a confirmed 1,654 deployed warheads and 792 deployed launchers.[45] The United States, however, can maintain stable deterrence while reducing strategic delivery vehicles by fifty percent from the Strategic Arms Reduction Treaty I level, and by reducing accountable strategic warheads by thirty percent from the Moscow Treaty level. The United States agrees with the New Strategic Arms Reduction Treaty limits by 2018 of:

- 1,550 accountable deployed strategic warheads
- 700 deployed strategic delivery vehicles
- A combined limit of 800 deployed and non-deployed strategic launchers

The United States also proposes reducing the number of accountable strategic warheads to slightly over 1,000.[46] The United States desires to maintain the current Nuclear Triad of intercontinental ballistic missiles, submarine-launched ballistic missiles, and nuclear-capable heavy bombers. All intercontinental ballistic missiles will only contain a single warhead each to increase strategic stability.[47] Finally, the United States will maintain the capability to forward-deploy nuclear weapons with heavy bombers and dual-capable aircraft.[48]

Further, recent nuclear employment strategic guidance outlines the following hedges against technical or geopolitical risk with fewer total nuclear weapons:[49]

- The United States will maintain a sufficient number of non-deployed nuclear weapons to hedge against technical failure of any single weapon type or delivery system

- Maintain legacy weapons to hedge against failure of weapons undergoing life-extension
- The non-deployed hedge stockpile of nuclear weapons provides the capability to upload additional weapons in response to changing geopolitical developments altering an assessment of deployed force requirements

Recent indications from the Obama Administration suggest that the United States will seek to further cut its nuclear force levels in size by roughly a third.[50] Officials are looking at a cut that would take the nuclear arsenal of deployed weapons to just above 1,000.[51] Senior Pentagon officials argue that a reduction to 900 warheads would still guarantee American safety, even if the United States only deployed half of them.[52] Whatever number the United States eventually settles on, the United States commits to maintaining a safe, secure, and effective nuclear arsenal,[53] providing the required capabilities to achieve the following ends:[54]

- Nuclear deterrence and strategic stability
- Extended deterrence
- Assuring United States allies and partners

GRAND, SECURITY, AND NUCLEAR WEAPONS STRATEGIES OF THE UNITED KINGDOM

The grand strategy of the United Kingdom is to accept a subordinate position without being simply another ally of the United States. This allows the United Kingdom to maintain global influence based on its ability to prompt the use of United States military forces in its interests.[55]

To achieve this goal, the United Kingdom needed to meet several geopolitical imperatives. The United Kingdom had to align with the United States-dominated alliance system and post-World War II financial arrangements lumped together under the Bretton Woods system. The United Kingdom needed to outstrip other United States allies both in the quantity of its military resources and in its willingness to use them at the behest of the United States. The United Kingdom had to maintain a full-spectrum military force, smaller than the United States military, but more capable across the board than the militaries of other allies of the United States.[56] The United Kingdom's current geopolitical imperative is two-fold:

- The United Kingdom has to maintain a balance of power between the United States and Europe
- The United Kingdom has to simultaneously maintain a balance of power on the European continent, especially one in which London has some degree of influence

Throughout its history, the United Kingdom's foremost concern was the emergence of a single European power that could threaten the British Isles politically, economically, or militarily. Thus, for the United Kingdom to maintain a balance of power, it has to accept reversal, retain autonomy, and accommodate itself to its environment while manipulating it.[57]

How does the security strategy of the United Kingdom meet its grand strategy goals? The United Kingdom's National Security Strategy has two clear objectives:[58]

- To ensure a secure and resilient United Kingdom by protecting its people, economy, infrastructure, territory, and ways of life from all major risks that can affect Britain directly
- To shape a stable world, by acting to reduce the likelihood of risks affecting the United Kingdom or its interests overseas, and applying all of its instruments of power and influence to shape the global environment and tackle potential risks at their source

To achieve these goals, the United Kingdom will:[59]

- Identify and monitor national security risks and opportunities
- Tackle the root causes of instability
- Exert influence to exploit opportunities and manage risks
- Enforce domestic law and strengthen international norms to help tackle those who threaten the United Kingdom and its interests
- Protect the United Kingdom and its interests at home, at its border, and internationally, to address physical and electronic threats from state and non-state sources
- Help resolve conflicts and contribute to stability
- Provide resilience for the United Kingdom by preparing for all kinds of emergencies
- Work in alliances and partnerships wherever possible to generate stronger responses

The United Kingdom identifies seven core military tasks that facilitate achieving its goals:[60]

- Defending the United Kingdom and its overseas territories
- Providing strategic intelligence
- Providing nuclear deterrence
- Supporting civil emergency organizations in times of crisis
- Defending its interests by projecting power strategically and through expeditionary interventions
- Providing a defense contribution to allies to exert British influence
- Providing security for stabilization

How does the nuclear weapons strategy of the United Kingdom meet its security strategy goals? The United Kingdom has the need for a minimum effective nuclear deterrent as the ultimate means to deter the most extreme threats. This nuclear deterrent supports collective security through the North Atlantic Treaty Organization for the Euro-Atlantic area. Nuclear deterrence plays an important part in the Alliance's overall strategy and Britain's nuclear forces make a substantial contribution to that deterrence.[61]

The United Kingdom would only consider using nuclear weapons in extreme circumstances of self-defense, including the defense of North Atlantic Treaty Organization allies. The United Kingdom remains deliberately ambiguous about precisely when, how, and at what scale it would contemplate the use of nuclear weapons. At the same time, the United Kingdom also remains committed to the long-term goal of a world without nuclear weapons. As such, the United Kingdom will not use or threaten to use nuclear weapons against non-nuclear weapon state parties to the Non-Proliferation Treaty.[62]

To preserve its nuclear deterrent, the United Kingdom will maintain a continuous submarine-based deterrent and begin the work of replacing its existing submarines. Due to fiscal constraints and a need for value for money, the United Kingdom believes it can meet the minimum requirement of an effective and credible level of deterrence with a smaller nuclear weapons capability. Thus, the United Kingdom will:[63]

- Reduce the number of warheads onboard each submarine from 48 to 40
- Reduce the requirement for operationally available warheads from fewer than 160 to no more than 120
- Reduce the overall nuclear weapon stockpile from not more than 225[64] to not more than 180 by the mid-2020s
- Reduce the number of operational missiles on each submarine to no more than eight

GRAND, SECURITY, AND NUCLEAR WEAPONS STRATEGIES OF FRANCE

As both a Northern and a Southern European power, the grand strategy of France is to attempt to project power and engage in all portions of the European theater. This allows France to maintain a degree of regional and global influence in excess of their actual hard and soft power capabilities.[65] To achieve this goal, France needs to meet several geopolitical imperatives:[66]

- Secure its larger hinterland
- Always look to the East for potential threats
- Maintain its influence in regions beyond Europe
- Be flexible in its policies in order to maximize its influence based on temporal circumstances

The greatest challenge for France in achieving its goals is safeguarding its Eastern border on the path of the historic invasion route through the North European Plain. In the past, France attempted this through a series of military conflicts. Currently, France achieves this imperative by aligning with Germany within the framework of the European Union.[67]

How does the security strategy of France meet its grand strategy goals? France seeks to be in a position where it does not have to submit to the effects of uncertainty. France strives to have the capacity to anticipate, respond to, and influence international developments. To achieve these goals, France will:[68]

- Leverage revolutions in knowledge and information
- Prevent or deter the risk of war
- Guarantee the security of its citizens as effectively as possible, both on French soil and beyond

France has a nested national security strategy, similar to the European Union's European Security Strategy.[69] The aim of France's National Security Strategy is to ward off risks or threats liable to harm the life of the nation by defending the population and French territory. Once France achieves this goal, the next imperative is to enable France to contribute to European and international security. Finally, exporting further abroad beyond Europe, the final aim is to defend the values that bind all French people to the State:[70]

- Principles of democracy
- Individual and collective freedoms
- Respect for human dignity, solidarity, and justice

France will achieve these aims through prevention and deterrence, and protection and intervention. Prevention averts or limits the occurrence of threats or wars that could target France directly or via a chain reaction. Deterrence prevents any State from thinking that it could attack the vital interests of France without incurring unacceptable risks for itself. Protection and intervention enable the State to ensure the security of its citizens, of its society, and of the economic life of the country. It is the combination of these different functions that ensures French national security.[71]

In its 2013 *French Defense White Paper*, France commits to pursuing further defense personnel and armament reductions, without negatively impacting its core nuclear deterrence mission or its aspirations for global relevance.[72] The *White Paper* identifies five main functions through which French military power can contribute to the attainment of France's strategic objectives:[73]

- Protection of the national territory and the preservation of France's independence and sovereignty
- Ensuring the ongoing stability of Europe and the North Atlantic space
- Increasing responsibility for taking the lead in providing security in the Guinea-to-Somalia stretch of territory
- Strengthening of military ties in the Near East and Persian Gulf
- Continue playing a role in global security

How does the nuclear weapons strategy of France meet its security strategy goals? Nuclear deterrence remains one of the foundations of France's strategy as the ultimate guarantee of national security and independence. Nuclear deterrence is strictly defensive. Its sole function is to prevent a state-originated aggression against the vital interests of the country, from whatever direction and in whatever form. The use of nuclear weapons would be conceivable only in extreme circumstances of self-defense. Thus, France maintains the capacity to deliver a nuclear warning within the framework of its policy of deterrence.[74]

France's strategy of deterrence also takes into account its alliances and developments in the construction of Europe. Significantly, together with the other European nuclear power, the United Kingdom, France notes that there is no situation in which the vital interests of one may be threatened without the interests of the other being threatened also. By its very existence, the French nuclear deterrent also contributes to the security of Europe. Within the Atlantic Alliance, the British and French nuclear forces contribute to global deterrence, a contribution recognized since 1974, and reiterated in the North Atlantic Treaty Organization's *Strategic Concept* of 1999.[75]

Although France retains a nuclear deterrent, France commits to nuclear disarmament. Together with the United Kingdom, it signed and ratified the Comprehensive Nuclear Test Ban Treaty. It closed and dismantled its facilities for the production of fissile material for explosive purposes at its nuclear test site in the Pacific. It dismantled its land-based nuclear missiles. It voluntarily reduced the number of its nuclear missile-launching submarines by a third. In the name of the principle of strict sufficiency, France also reduced by a third the number of nuclear weapons, missiles, and aircraft in its airborne component. With these reductions, France's nuclear arsenal comprises fewer than 300 warheads,[76] which is half the maximum number of warheads it held during the Cold War.[77]

The operational credibility of France's nuclear deterrent relies on permanent submarine patrols and airborne capability. The naval forces provide the permanent presence at sea of the strategic submarine force (six nuclear attack submarines), guaranteeing a second-strike deterrent capability. The weapons carried by both components are of a strategic nature. In no way do they constitute battlefield weapons for military use in theater. In 2010, an intercontinental ballistic missile was brought into service, providing the seaborne component with a much extended range and increased flexibility. In 2009, France equipped the airborne component with cruise missiles deployed on aircraft stationed in France or carrier-based. France will continue to maintain its nuclear forces at a level of strict sufficiency and will constantly scale them at the lowest possible level compatible with its security.[78] Projected future budgetary constraints also contribute to France's desire to maintain its nuclear deterrence capability with the minimal level of financial resource investment.[79]

The preservation of the airborne and submarine components of its nuclear deterrent, and the ongoing commitment to defense industrial and technological autonomy, confirm the French nuclear force as the centerpiece of French grand strategy. They also reaffirm France's strong desire for military and strategic autonomy.[80]

GRAND, SECURITY, AND NUCLEAR WEAPONS STRATEGIES OF THE NORTH ATLANTIC TREATY ORGANIZATION

The grand strategy of the North Atlantic Treaty Organization is to ensure that the Alliance remains an unparalleled community of freedom, peace, security, and shared values. To achieve this vision, the Alliance will:[81]

- Defend allied nations
- Deploy robust military forces where and when required for security
- Promote common security around the globe

To achieve these goals, the North Atlantic Treaty Organization commits to meeting several geopolitical imperatives. First and foremost, the Alliance's enduring purpose is to safeguard the freedom and security of all its members by political and military means. The Alliance is firmly committed to the purposes and principles of the Charter of the United Nations. In order to assure the security of its members, the Alliance will continue fulfilling effectively three essential core tasks:

- Collective defense
- Crisis management
- Cooperative security

Finally, the Allies will engage in a continuous process of reform, modernization, and transformation to carry out the full range of North Atlantic Treaty Organization missions as effectively and efficiently as possible.[82]

How does the security strategy of the North Atlantic Treaty Organization meet its grand strategy goals? The greatest responsibility of the Alliance is to protect and defend its territory and populations against attack. To do this, the Alliance will ensure it has the full range of capabilities necessary to deter and defend against any threat to the safety and security of its populations. The Alliance will achieve security through effective crisis management. The Alliance will promote international security through cooperation, supporting arms control, disarmament, and non-proliferation efforts. Additionally, the Alliance will attempt to achieve its security strategy goals by seeking further enlargement and promoting further Euro-Atlantic security partnerships. Finally, the Alliance will pursue reform and transformation to become the premier alliance of the twenty-first century.[83]

How does the nuclear weapons strategy of the North Atlantic Treaty Organization meet its security strategy goals? The Alliance resolves to seek a safer world for all and to create the conditions for a world without nuclear weapons in accordance with the goals of the Non-Proliferation Treaty, in a way that promotes international stability, based on the principle of undiminished security for all. The proliferation of nuclear weapons and other weapons of mass destruction threaten incalculable consequences for global stability and prosperity. Thus, the Alliance countries commit the organization to the goal of creating the conditions for a world without nuclear weapons. The Alliance reconfirms, however, that as long as there are nuclear weapons in the world, the North Atlantic Treaty Organization will remain a nuclear alliance. Deterrence, based on an appropriate mix of nuclear and conventional capabilities, remains a core element of the Alliance's overall strategy, even though circumstances in which the Alliance might use nuclear weapons are extremely remote.[84]

The strategic nuclear forces of the Alliance, particularly those of the United States, are the supreme guarantee of the security of the allies. The independent strategic nuclear forces of the United Kingdom and France, which have a deterrent role of their own, contribute to the overall deterrence and security of the allies. Thus, the North Atlantic Treaty Organization commits to maintaining an appropriate mix of nuclear and conventional forces. The Allies also commit to ensuring the broadest possible participation of allies in collective defense planning on nuclear roles, in peacetime basing of nuclear forces, and in command, control, and consultation arrangements. With the changes in the security environment since the end of the Cold War, the North Atlantic Treaty Organization has dramatically reduced the number of nuclear weapons stationed in Europe and its reliance on nuclear weapons in Alliance strategy. The North Atlantic Treaty Organization seeks to create the conditions for further reductions in the future.[85]

GRAND, SECURITY, AND NUCLEAR WEAPONS STRATEGIES OF THE EUROPEAN UNION

The grand strategy of the European Union is to achieve full economic, and eventually political, integration of all European community nation-states. The European Union's position is that multilateral engagement is the preeminent tool for solving major strategic problems.[86]

To achieve this goal, the European Union needs to meet several geopolitical imperatives. First and foremost, the European Union must keep the peace on the European continent. Only when Europeans assure peace on the continent, can the Europeans then turn toward attempting to remake the international liberal world order based on effective multilateral engagement, with the European Union as the example for the global community to emulate. Ultimately, the goal of the European Union is to achieve its ultimate vision of world peace.[87]

Lacking full political integration, however, the European Union is only marginally successful at exporting its strategy beyond the boundaries of Europe. The European Union itself is fragmenting due to diverging national interests and differing conceptions of multilateralism among its member states.[88]

How does the security strategy of the European Union meet its grand strategy goals? The European Union sees its existence as proof of a transformation in the relationship between States that led to peace and stability in Europe. The European Union commits to peacefully settling disputes and cooperating through common institutions. The rule of law and democracy created a united and peaceful continent. The European Union sees this model as its vision for the world. Europe still faces threats and challenges, but Europeans see the future of conflict as an intra–state issue and not the traditional threat of state versus state warfare.[89]

The European Union does not take a strategic approach to meeting its top security priorities. The European Union fails to articulate any overarching priorities because there is no common consensus within the European Union on a shared strategic vision with associated enduring European interests. Instead, the European Union outlines some strategic objectives narrowly focused on addressing the outlined threats. The European Union dispenses with the traditional concept of self–defense against the threat of invasion, and posits the first line of defense abroad, advocating acting before crises occur.[90]

To achieve conflict and threat prevention, the European Union will build security along its borders in its near periphery and promote an international order based on effective multilateralism. The European Union will advance these policies:[91]

- By becoming more active in pursuing strategic objectives in a cooperative multilateral environment
- By becoming more capable across the spectrum of the instruments of power
- By more coherently articulating common foreign, security, and defense policies
- By working with partners in a cooperative multilateral environment

Does the European Union have a nuclear weapons strategy to meet its security strategy goals? In short, the answer is no. Conspicuously absent in the European Union's security strategy is any direct mention of military force as a means to achieve objectives, much less a mention of nuclear weapons in achieving these objectives. The European Union commits to improving military capabilities and to maintaining defensive alliances and relationships. The European Union makes little commitment, however, as to how, when, or if military force plays a role in advancing European Union strategic security objectives. The key European Union member countries in question, the United Kingdom and France, leave it to the North Atlantic Treaty Organization to answer those questions.

SUMMARY

Strategically, future nuclear coalition operations seem feasible. The allied nations in question, the United States, the United Kingdom, and France, as well as their collective security alliance, the North Atlantic Treaty Organization, share similar strategies regarding nuclear weapons policies and thus nuclear coalition operationalization is possible. Although the European Union appears to be an outlier regarding nuclear weapons policy, for the nations that belong to both the European Union and to the North Atlantic Treaty Organization, all defer to the North Atlantic Treaty Organization regarding strategic defense issues. Thus, synergies exist in the nuclear weapons policies of these security community allies in the following areas:

Strategic Defense

- Promoting strategic stability
- Supporting collective security and global deterrence
- Credibly guaranteeing defense commitments with tailored deterrence capabilities
- Preventing nuclear proliferation and nuclear terrorism

Current Role of Nuclear Weapons

- Guaranteeing national security and independence, even though circumstances in which any use of nuclear weapons might occur are extremely remote
- Deterring nuclear attack on the homeland or on allies and partners is the sole purpose of nuclear weapons
- Committing to not using or threatening to use nuclear weapons against non-nuclear weapon states that are party to and in compliance with the Nuclear Non-Proliferation Treaty

Size of Nuclear Weapons Arsenals and Force Structure

- Sustaining a safe, secure, and effective nuclear arsenal
- Maintaining strategic deterrence and stability at reduced nuclear force levels
- Preserving a minimum effective nuclear deterrent as the ultimate means to deter the most extreme threats
- Maintaining nuclear forces at a level of strict sufficiency, constantly scaled at the lowest possible level compatible with security
- Committing to multiple delivery mechanisms as necessary (sea, air, & land)

Future Role of Nuclear Weapons

- Reducing the role and numbers of nuclear weapons
- Moving step-by-step toward eliminating nuclear weapons
- Committing to nuclear disarmament and the long-term goal of a world without nuclear weapons

Role of Nuclear Coalition Operations

- Helping allies build deterrent capacities to enhance regional and global security
- As long as there are nuclear weapons in the world, the North Atlantic Treaty Organization, and bilateral/trilateral alliances, will remain nuclear alliances
- Broadest possible participation of allies in collective defense planning on nuclear roles, in peacetime basing of nuclear forces, and in command, control, and consultation arrangements
- There is no situation in which the vital interests of one nation may be threatened without the interests of the others being threatened also

NUCLEAR COALITION OPERATIONS AT THE OPERATIONAL LEVEL

Clearly, a future Trilateral Nuclear Force comprising the United States, the United Kingdom, and France is theoretically possible given the synergies between the three nations on strategic defense and nuclear weapons policies. One might even say it is theoretically likely once the United States reduces its nuclear arsenal to levels equal to that of its Euro-Atlantic allies, given the numerous fiscal and operational constraints in maintaining the requirements of such a force at lower numbers. The question remains though – How to operationalize this synergy at the strategic level into a functional force structure at the operational level?

Coalition operations in Europe are now the norm across the military spectrum. The European Union entertained considerable debate in the last decade over the issue of defense procurement in an effort to increase integration as part of a larger expansion in Common Security and Defense Policy.[92] After the European financial crisis of 2008, the concept of pooling and sharing of military capabilities became preeminent policy within the European Union[93] as a means of facilitating military cooperation to survive austerity measures.[94]

One excellent example of successful pooling and sharing was the creation of the European Defense Agency. Established in 2004, and modified in 2011, the European Defense Agency's mission is to improve the European Union's defense capabilities, in a pragmatic, cost effective, and results-oriented manner, offering multinational solutions for capability improvement in a time when defense budget constraints foster a need for cooperation. The European Defense Agency's focus on capabilities provides an integrated approach to delivering warfighter needs by shaping the defense technological and industrial base across the European Union.[95] The European Defense Agency is just one example of the rise of European security cooperation.[96]

What of cooperation specifically between the United Kingdom and France? The United Kingdom and France are the European Union's two most dominant global military powers and are the only nuclear powers in the European Union. Together, the United Kingdom and France account for forty percent of Europe's defense budget, fifty percent of its military capacity, and seventy percent of all spending in military research and development.[97] In 2010, the United Kingdom and France signed the Lancaster House Treaties for security and defense cooperation. These two bilateral treaties declared elements of cooperation in the following areas:[98]

- Defense and security cooperation
- Nuclear stockpile stewardship
- Operational matters
- Industry and armaments
- Equipment and capabilities
- Counter-terrorism

They also agreed to create a combined Joint Expeditionary Force and an integrated United Kingdom-French aircraft carrier strike group.[99] The French, however, backed off building the joint aircraft carrier due to budgetary constraints.[100]

Clearly, the United Kingdom and France are not only in synch in terms of strategic policy, but are capable of cooperative coalition operations at the operational level as well.[101] In their most recent *Defense White Paper*, France reiterates its commitment to the North Atlantic Treaty Organization, the security of the European Union, as well as its enhanced defense-relationship with the United Kingdom on matters of mutual defense and security cooperation.[102]

The United Kingdom and France exhibit similar levels of cooperation regarding nuclear weapons issues. The 2010 Lancaster House Treaties will pool the resources of the armed forces of both nations to maintain their status as major global defense powers. The United Kingdom and France will also work jointly with nuclear weapons. France and the United Kingdom will carry out testing in France, and the United Kingdom and France will develop technology in the United Kingdom.[103] Both nations agree to collaboration on the technology associated with nuclear stockpile stewardship in support of both countries' independent nuclear deterrent capabilities, including a new joint facility at Valduc in France that will model performance of nuclear warheads and materials to ensure long-term viability, security, and safety. A joint Technology Development Center at Aldermaston in the United Kingdom will support this effort.[104]

In addition, the United Kingdom and France are exploring further mutual security confidence building measures. Through shadow declarations, the United Kingdom and France could provide data consistent with certain specific data exchanged between the United States and Russia under the New Strategic Arms Reduction Treaty. The United Kingdom and France might also consider broader declarations with respect to future plans for their nuclear forces. Data exchanges on strategic forces would be an important step towards building increased transparency, cooperation, and trust among all nuclear-weapon states in the Euro-Atlantic region.[105]

What about cooperation between the United States and these two European allies? These three nations ground their framework for transatlantic cooperation firmly in the North Atlantic Treaty Organization Alliance. Thus, in the short-term, any further cooperation will develop within the Atlantic Alliance framework. Substantial debate is ongoing across the Atlantic about the operational role of nuclear weapons within the North Atlantic Treaty Organization Alliance. The recent North Atlantic Treaty Organization Strategic Concept reconfirmed, however, that as long as there are nuclear weapons in the world, the North Atlantic Treaty Organization will remain a nuclear alliance.[106]

The Atlantic alliance has a long history of successful cooperation on issues involving nuclear weapons. Nuclear sharing is a concept in the North Atlantic Treaty Organization's policy of nuclear deterrence, which involves member countries without nuclear weapons of their own in the planning for the use of nuclear weapons by the North Atlantic Treaty Organization, and in particular provides for involvement of the armed forces of these countries in delivering these weapons in the event of their use. As part of nuclear sharing, the participating countries carry out consultations and take common decisions on nuclear weapons policy, maintain technical equipment required for the use of nuclear weapons (including aircraft capable of delivering them), and store nuclear weapons on their territory. Of the three nuclear powers in the North Atlantic Treaty Organization, however, only the United States provides weapons for nuclear sharing.[107] In the New Concept, members pledge to ensure the broadest possible participation of allies in collective defense planning on nuclear roles, in peacetime basing of nuclear forces, and in command, control, and consultation arrangements.[108]

The North Atlantic Treaty Organization's Nuclear Planning Group is another example of cooperation. The senior institution on nuclear policy issues, the Nuclear Planning Group acts as the senior body on nuclear matters in the Alliance. The Defense Ministers of all member countries, except France, meet at regular intervals, where they discuss specific policy issues associated with nuclear forces. The Alliance's nuclear policy is kept under review and decisions are taken jointly to modify or adapt policies in the light of new developments and to update and adjust planning and consultation procedures.[109] France, which had left the North Atlantic Treaty Organization's integrated military structure in 1966, returned in 2010, but it does not yet participate in the Nuclear Planning Group. France wants its nuclear deterrent to remain to a degree independent of the Alliance.[110]

Although the allies firmly ground short-term nuclear cooperation and thus nuclear deterrence in the North Atlantic Treaty Organizational framework,[111] several notable national security practitioners agree that the future of nuclear deterrence in Europe in the long-term will rely on independent deterrence or on nuclear coalition operations on a bilateral or trilateral basis.[112] Michel even argues that closer cooperation among the three allies will allow France and the United Kingdom to more effectively manage the current period of defense austerity, while leaving their highest-leverage defense capabilities intact.[113] Clearly, the United States, the United Kingdom, and France are at the very least exploring possible avenues for maintaining current levels of deterrence in the future given likely future arms reductions and continued future fiscal austerity.[114]

SUMMARY

Undoubtedly, there is much consensus at the operational level as well between the United Kingdom and France bilaterally, and between the United States, the United Kingdom, and France trilaterally within the context of the North Atlantic Treaty Organization. Nuclear weapons are likely to remain in Europe in the context of the Atlantic Alliance in at least the short term.[115] In the long term, however, as pressures for arms reductions continue, the nuclear allies are likely to retain their sovereign deterrent options, but in a severely constrained environment both in terms of the lower number of nuclear weapons deployable and in terms of the fiscal and operational constraints required to maintain the same levels of deterrence at much lower numbers.

The Allies face several external challenges into the future, with significant implications for strategic stability:[116]

- Increased complexity of deterrence relationships
- Dispersion of weapons of mass destruction to new actors capable of disrupting regional or global stability
- Increased strategic significance of Asia

The Allies also face internal threats to their cohesion:[117]

- Disputes over unequal burden-sharing and risk-sharing arrangements
- Differing threat perceptions among North Atlantic Treaty Organization members
- Varying approaches to managing Alliance-wide defense drawdowns

Yet despite both external and internal threats to Alliance relationships, a degree of unity exists among the United States, the United Kingdom, and France on a variety of nuclear issues:[118]

- Defining the role of nuclear weapons within cross domain deterrent relationships
- Promoting non-proliferation efforts
- Advancing the North Atlantic Treaty Organization's nuclear policy
- Enhancing material security

Thus, this analysis suggests that the foundation already exists for future nuclear coalition operations between these allies. If a Trilateral Force is feasible at both the strategic and operational levels, what sort for future force structure might it take?

FORCE STRUCTURE OPTIONS FOR THE CONFIGURATION OF A FUTURE TRILATERAL FORCE

Although this analysis demonstrates that a future Trilateral Force is not only feasible, but likely, from both strategic and operational perspectives, the discussion becomes more difficult when analyzing force structure. For it is with decisions about force structure, when nations have to obligate tangible money against intangible policies, where we can truly gauge how much sovereignty the allies in question would be willing to relinquish to cooperative coalitions.

For nuclear coalition operations, it seems clear that some combination of the Nuclear Triad is the likely future force structure, whether as a Trilateral Force or as independent sovereign nations. All things being equal, the United States, the United Kingdom, and France would all agree that the preferred force structure for their nuclear forces would be a robust Nuclear Triad of sea based submarine-launched ballistic missiles, land based intercontinental ballistic missiles, and nuclear capable fighters and bombers. All things are not equal, and each of these nations has to make decisions based on a number of factors. The two most important are:

- Fiscal constraints
- The efficiencies of operational feasibility, or lack thereof, at lower numbers

These two issues are mutually reinforcing. Continued declines in defense budgets will make it difficult for the United States to maintain a robust Nuclear Triad, while the United Kingdom (only submarines) and France (submarines and aircraft) already do not maintain a Triad. Part of why they do not is not just cost, but also the infeasibility of maintaining all three legs when their numbers of nuclear weapons are between 200-300 warheads. The United States will face the same dilemma of the feasibility of maintaining its Nuclear Triad once arms reductions take its nuclear arsenal below 500 warheads. Both of these constraints are primary drivers conditioning the likelihood that these three allies will turn to a future Trilateral Force to mitigate these constraints.

Taking these two constraints into consideration, I offer the following options for the force structure of a future Trilateral Nuclear Force.

FORCE STRUCTURE OPTIONS

Option 1: All three nations utilize and maintain all three legs of the Nuclear Triad

Although this would be the preferred option of all three nations in an ideal world, it is the least likely option for implementation. Neither the United Kingdom nor France maintains land-based intercontinental ballistic missiles. The United Kingdom no longer employs nuclear capable aircraft. It seems highly unlikely that either nation would add these legs of the Nuclear Triad, even given complete integration with the United States. At lower numbers of overall nuclear warheads (less than 1,000 for the

Trilateral Force), the operational inefficiencies at lower numbers, coupled with prohibitive costs, make this a non-viable option.

Option 2: All three nations maintain the same two legs of the Nuclear Triad

Global Zero argues that a notional United States force structure by 2022 would consist of ten Trident ballistic missile submarines armed with 720 strategic missile warheads and 18 B-2 bombers armed with 180 gravity bombs. The United States would eliminate the Minuteman land-based intercontinental ballistic missile force and all tactical nuclear weapons.[119] This would leave the United States with a Dyad of submarines and bombers. The French already employ this force structure. This option would only require the United Kingdom to reconstitute a small fleet of nuclear bomb capable aircraft, a transition that a nuclear capable air Wing of the United States Air Force already stationed in Great Britain could easily facilitate. The United States would reap enormous savings from eliminating the intercontinental ballistic missile force, and all three nations would reap savings and gain operational efficiencies by eliminating tactical nuclear weapons and integrating their respective submarine and aircraft fleets. This appears to be a viable option.

Option 3: All three nations maintain two different legs of the Nuclear Triad

The obvious benefit of this option would be the maintenance of the entire Triad within the Trilateral Force with redundancy at each leg, but at less cost than maintaining the entire Triad for all three nations. Based on the current capabilities for each nation, this notional force structure would see the United States maintaining its intercontinental ballistic missile force and bomber fleet, France maintaining its current Dyad of submarines and aircraft, and the United Kingdom maintaining its submarines and constituting an intercontinental ballistic missile force. There is a reason, however, that neither the French nor the British maintain an intercontinental ballistic missile force. The biggest advantages of the intercontinental ballistic missile leg of the Triad are its long-range strategic strike capabilities and its survivability in the face of a first strike due to its dispersed nature, if maintained in sufficient numbers. With the assumption that the Russians also continue to draw down their nuclear stockpile for the same reasons as outlined for the West, the future nuclear landscape is unlikely to require a need to deter and prevail over peer adversaries requiring survivability and the ability to defeat defenses to ensure a devastating response to an adversary's first strike. Also, neither the United Kingdom nor France possesses a large enough territory commensurate with the United States to make dispersal and thus survivability effective. Thus, the future nuclear landscape suggests that the intercontinental ballistic missile leg of the Triad will be the least valuable of the three. Consequently, this is not a likely option as it would require either France or the United Kingdom to constitute an intercontinental ballistic missile force. In addition, the United States is highly unlikely to relinquish its submarine fleet to meet the requirements of this option.

Option 4: All three nations maintain only one, single leg of the Nuclear Triad

The only leg of the Triad that all three nations currently employ is submarines. Thus, submarine-launched ballistic missiles are the logical choice for this option. Kingston and colleagues make some sound arguments in favor of this option. Nuclear submarines are the most valued leg of the Triad for the United States; while the Russians value their intercontinental ballistic missile force the most. This suggests that nuclear capable aircraft will be the first leg eliminated in further rounds of nuclear arms reduction negotiations and treaties between the two nations. In addition, the inherent vulnerability of immobile intercontinental ballistic missiles creates destabilizing "use or lose" pressures and thus the desire to draw down this leg as well. Submarine-launched ballistic missiles can provide the credible deterrence maintenance needed to eventually eliminate the need for intercontinental ballistic missiles. As pressures mount for future reductions to all three legs of the Triad to achieve minimum deterrence, a safe and secure submarine-launched ballistic missile force seems destined to remain the centerpiece of deterrence into the future.[120]

On the other hand, Lowther convincingly argues that this Monad does not have the capability and credibility to create the desired psychological effect to achieve effective deterrence. Eliminating the bomber leg of the Triad would diminish the vital capability to signal intent. The expense of intercontinental ballistic missiles prohibitively raises the cost of entry for potential proliferators, while their strong counterstrike ability increases risks for adversaries. Finally, if half the submarine fleet is in port at any given time, as a Monad they become more vulnerable to attack.[121]

It seems that this option is less desirable in the early stages of nuclear coalition operations, while peer competitors like Russia still maintain large nuclear weapons stockpiles. In the later stages of nuclear weapons reductions, however, when all nuclear weapons states resemble global or regional actors with much smaller nuclear arsenals, the situation is different. During the period between reaching global nuclear parity and eventual global nuclear zero, a Trilateral Force consisting of a Monad of submarine-launched ballistic missiles would achieve a level of deterrence superiority at economies of scale.

Option 5: Each nation maintains a single, different leg of the Nuclear Triad

The obvious benefit of this option is that the Trilateral Force is able to collectively maintain the benefits of the entire Triad without each individual nation incurring the costs of maintaining all three legs of the Triad. The United States would maintain its intercontinental ballistic missile force since it is the only nation of the three which currently has an intercontinental ballistic missile force. The United Kingdom would maintain its submarine fleet since it currently has a Monad force structure. Finally, France would maintain a nuclear capable aircraft fleet to complete the Trilateral Force Triad.

Strategically, this option makes the most sense, as it would meet the synergistic elements of all three nations' security strategies with the least cost. Operationally and tactically, it would be the most difficult option to implement. Where would the Alliance draw the line between sovereignty and collective security? Would each nation trust the other two to use nuclear force against an enemy they might not share the same threat perception of if a nation deemed an ally's leg of the Triad best suited for utilization in a particular scenario? France currently keeps its nuclear deterrent to a degree independent of its alliance structures. It seems unlikely that France would reduce the sovereignty of its nuclear options in the future to this level of integration. The United States also would be unlikely to cede operational control over elements of its nuclear deterrent to this degree in this fashion.

Option 6: The United States maintains its Nuclear Triad, supplemented with United Kingdom and French capabilities

A recent report by the Center for Strategic and International Studies almost universally recommends that the United States should maintain its current nuclear posture (the Triad) regardless of how low the United States goes in reducing its overall nuclear arsenal.[122] The United States should maintain nuclear forces at the lowest levels necessary to meet its deterrence, assurance, and defense requirements. For the foreseeable future, the United States should sustain a strategic Triad of delivery systems and dual-capable fighters, as these capabilities meet important strategic objectives and mitigate risk. The authors argue that there is no overriding economic, political, or strategic advantage in eliminating any leg of the Triad or nuclear-capable fighter aircraft.[123]

Blechman argues that the United States needs to maintain overall nuclear capabilities that are at least comparable to any potential adversary for the foreseeable future.[124] Brooks argues that the United States should maintain the Nuclear Triad for at least another twenty years.[125] DeGrasse argues that the current Triad of strategic nuclear delivery systems provides options that enhance strategic stability and thus the United States should maintain the Triad for the immediate future.[126] Joseph argues that the flexibility, diversity, and resilience that derive from the Triad are essential to meet changing security threats over time.[127] Finally, Klotz argues that the triad still has intrinsic, enduring value, particularly at lower numbers. It provides a balanced mix of desirable attributes, including responsiveness, survivability, ability to penetrate defenses, and the ability to signal resolve. It mitigates against the risks of a failure of a single warhead or delivery system, targeted investment by other nations to counter one or more of the legs, and unforeseen changes in the strategic environment. Finally, it also contributes to strategic stability by presenting any would-be adversary with an insurmountably complex targeting problem and thereby reducing any incentive to launch a first strike.[128]

The only slightly dissenting opinion comes from Perkovich. He argues that the United States should fund extension of the Minuteman force through 2030, rather than commit now to a new replacement for the intercontinental ballistic missile force. During the next fifteen years, the United

States should thus prepare to move to a Dyad nuclear force structure based on submarine-launched ballistic missiles and bombers.[129]

This option seems the most likely in the short-term. For the next generation, as further reductions in global nuclear arms proceeds apace, the United States can maintain a reducing Triad over time, while working to integrate further with its Atlantic allies to best prepare for a future when a Trilateral Force becomes the best, and maybe the only, option.

The three allies can begin merging less operationally and tactically sensitive aspects of their nuclear operations. For instance, the United States can integrate into the work the United Kingdom and France have already begun in merging their testing and nuclear stockpile stewardship. They can begin integrating research and development efforts and take steps toward integrated operational utilization. These initial steps would lay the foundation for a future Trilateral Force structure. Although this might be the preferred option in the short-term, it is not a viable option for the long-term future of nuclear global parity due to the costs involved and the eventual operational inefficiencies at much lower nuclear force levels.

SUMMARY

The following table summarizes the six options explored:

Table 1: Force Structure Options for a Future Trilateral Force

		Option 1	Option 2	Option 3	Option 4	Option 5	Option 6
United States	ICBMs	X		X		X	X
	SLBMs	X	X		X		X
	Aircraft	X	X	X			X
United Kingdom	ICBMs	X		X			
	SLBMs	X	X	X	X	X	X
	Aircraft	X	X				
France	ICBMs	X					
	SLBMs	X	X	X	X		X
	Aircraft	X	X	X		X	X

Each option has inherent positive aspects as well as negative repercussions. No single option fits the strategic needs of the United States across the spectrum from today's geopolitical realities to the hoped for future world of global zero. Thus, perhaps a phased force structure, that meets the needs of the present while preparing for the realities of the future, is the best approach.

During **Phase One** (*Option 6*), facing the current global nuclear environment, the United States should maintain its current Nuclear Triad force structure without investing in mass block modernization programs of the intercontinental ballistic missile force or bomber fleet. Instead those resources should divert to beginning integration programs with the United Kingdom and France. All three nations should maintain and modernize as necessary their submarine fleets, but with less of them with less missiles on them. The United States would maintain a smaller strategic intercontinental ballistic missile force, with perhaps some allied contributions toward the cost. This would conceivably last a generation.

During **Phase Two** (*Option 2*), nuclear arms control reductions would achieve a watershed moment where the world's nuclear powers reach relative nuclear parity. While the hard work is begun involving all nuclear weapons states in further reduction negotiations, the Trilateral Force would become operational, having integrated the three nations' nuclear research, technology, and development, stockpile management, and operational utilization. The Trilateral Force would begin the work of transitioning to a Dyad force structure. The United States would delete its intercontinental ballistic missiles altogether as the world geostrategic situation allows. All three nations would perhaps maintain a latent nuclear capability for aircraft, but with none on alert. This would conceivably last another generation.

Finally, during **Phase Three** (*Option 4*), the Trilateral Force, now fully operational and proven, would transition to a Monad force structure of submarine-launched ballistic missiles. This would allow the Alliance to maintain a degree of relative deterrence superiority as future global arms reductions take place, while reaping the benefits of cost savings and the efficiencies of integrated operations. This stage would again conceivably last a generation, until hopefully the allies could disband the Trilateral Force as the world reaches global zero at the dawn of the Twenty-Second Century.

The following table summarizes this phased approach:

Table 2: Force Structures Phases for a Future Trilateral Force

		Phase 1	Phase 2	Phase 3
United States	ICBMs	X		
	SLBMs	X	X	X
	Aircraft	X	X	
United Kingdom	ICBMs			
	SLBMs	X	X	X
	Aircraft		X	
France	ICBMs			
	SLBMs	X	X	X
	Aircraft	X	X	

CONCLUSIONS AND POLICY RECOMMENDATIONS

Current nuclear weapons strategy traps the United States in the policy paradox of desiring continued nuclear arms reductions while recognizing the current reality of needing to maintain a robust nuclear arms deterrent. Future United States nuclear weapons policy must balance the two imperatives of working toward a world free of nuclear weapons and retaining nuclear weapons to deter attack on the United States and its allies while nuclear weapons still exist.

As nuclear arms reduction efforts continue into the next generation, if the number of United States nuclear weapons drops to the level of its allies, the United Kingdom and France, the United States can still meet its security commitments and maintain a credible extended deterrence through nuclear coalition operations. The United States can continue to meet its security commitments, maintaining a credible extended deterrence, while reducing its nuclear arsenal to the minimum level required, achieving and maintaining strategic stability among the world's nuclear powers.

In the future, only through nuclear coalition operations can the United States continue to meet its national security commitments at minimum deterrence levels. Synergies exist in the nuclear weapons policies of United States security community allies to the extent that cooperation between the United States, the United Kingdom, and France can occur on the strategic, operational, and tactical levels. Thus, the proposed Trilateral Force is a viable means of maintaining a Nuclear Triad capable of meeting extended deterrence security commitments, while preserving strategic stability at the lowest possible nuclear arsenal levels, at the least cost and greatest efficiency.

A future Atlantic Alliance trilateral nuclear force structure between the three allies is a possible means to achieve shared national security objectives. The best option is a phased approach linking current and future force structure needs with arms reduction goals instead of considering the two issues in isolation. A Trilateral Force structure bridges seemingly opposing requirements of national security. It allows the United States to incrementally and continually reduce its nuclear arsenal in pursuit of arms reduction goals, preserving operational capability and strategic stability among the world's nuclear powers, while maintaining a credible minimal deterrence posture.

Nuclear coalition cooperation at the strategic level is not only viable, but essential among the three allies. Operationalizing a Trilateral Force structure, however, is a challenging proposition due to four overarching factors.

First, at the strategic level, retaining current policy synergies among the allies may prove extremely difficult without a shared existential threat perception. During the Cold War, the Atlantic Alliance firmly united its nuclear weapons policy in the face of the existential threat of the Soviet Union. In the post-Cold War world, the changing threat environment is slowly eroding the idea of Euro-Atlantic collective security as the individual national security interests of European states are diverging. The impact of diverging national security interests among European states on the cohesion and further development of European security cooperation suggests several potential outcomes, not all of which are synergistic with the interests of the United States, much less among the European states themselves.[130] The North Atlantic Treaty Organization's enlargement to the Baltic States combined with pro–Western Georgian and Ukrainian color revolutions jarred Russia into a resurgence, which is causing Central Europeans to recalculate their threat environment. By contrast, France and Germany do not want another Cold War splitting the continent. Add to this threat environment the severe European economic crisis, and it is clear that national security policy synergies among European allies are diminishing,[131] even among North Atlantic Treaty Organization member states.[132]

Second, if security strategy synergies fragment in the future, at the tactical level, would the United States, the United Kingdom, and France continue to agree on when and how to actually use nuclear weapons in a particular threat scenario? Currently, the United Kingdom and France explicitly, and the United States implicitly, at least concerning the Euro-Atlantic region, note that there is no situation in which the vital interests of one may be threatened without the interests of the others being threatened also.[133] The Allies must construct the Trilateral Force on this strategic bedrock as a foundation. Although it is difficult to imagine a scenario today in which one of the three countries would desire to use nuclear weapons and at least one of the other two would oppose it, such a scenario needs consideration when relinquishing a degree of sovereignty as part of operationalizing a Trilateral Force.

Third, the United States currently has larger extended deterrence commitments, than either the United Kingdom or France, with its East Asian allies. The Trilateral Force concept primarily explores the implications for Euro-Atlantic security, but clearly there are implications for East Asian security that need addressing as well from the United States perspective. Would the United Kingdom and France extend their deterrence capabilities to the East Asian allies of the United States? Would those East Asian allies accept those assurances? If not, is a Trilateral Force even a viable option for the United States? These questions are crucial to answer, but require an examination beyond the scope of this paper.

Finally, this phased approach assumes that Russia matches the United States with arms reductions down to the 300-500 nuclear warheads level, and assumes that China will engage in global arms control negotiations once the United States and Russia reach a level of parity with China. Both scenarios are feasible, but are by no means guaranteed based on the evolving geopolitical situation during the next generation. A shared threat perception among the larger nuclear powers, perhaps smaller regional nuclear powers like North Korea and Iran, would facilitate global arms reduction efforts. While diverging threat perceptions, perhaps Russia and China viewing each other as the primary threat, would stall further global arms reduction efforts. The geopolitical future is uncertain on this issue. In addition, it is likely that if Russia and China both agreed to participate in nuclear arms reductions down to global parity levels, both countries would view the emergence of a Trilateral Force in the West as a threat to strategic stability and thus they might halt any further reductions.

If the United States can mitigate these four areas of concern, then the recommendation for future United States nuclear weapons policy is to begin laying the groundwork for a future Trilateral Nuclear Force and link its further development to future continued arms control reductions. By linking an increase in nuclear coalition operations to a decrease in nuclear arsenals, the United States can bridge the gap between the desire for global zero and the need to maintain an effective nuclear deterrent.

Future research in this area should gear toward interviewing current nuclear policy decision makers in the United States, the United Kingdom, France, and the North Atlantic Treaty Organization to ascertain the feasibility of turning the phased approach model recommended here into executable national and coalition policy. From 2009-2013, the Center for Strategic and International Studies, with support from the Defense Threat Reduction Agency, institutionalized a trilateral Track 1.5/2 nuclear dialogue between former senior government officials and academics from the United States, the United Kingdom, and France, contributing to Allied unity on nuclear issues.[134] Future strategic dialogues should include the feasibility of institutionalizing a future Trilateral Force structure.

A Trilateral Force may not come into existence for a generation or more, but if the current arms control trajectory holds, the United States should promote and constitute such a Trilateral Force if it is to meet the challenges of a changing nuclear policy security environment during the approaching latter half of the Twenty-First Century. The time to start preparing is now.

ENDNOTES

[1] *Nuclear Posture Review Report* (2010), 9.

[2] Ibid., 41.

[3] Ibid., 43. See also Rose Gottemoeller, "New Strategic Arms Reduction Treaty: Security Through 21st-Century Verification," *Arms Control Today*, September (2010), 10.

[4] Robert Manning, *Envisioning 2030: U.S. Strategy for a Post-Western World*, Atlantic Council (2013), 46.

[5] Paul Bracken, *The Second Nuclear Age: Strategy, Danger, and the New Power Politics* (New York: Times Books, 2012).

[6] William Walker, *President-Elect Obama and Nuclear Disarmament: Between Elimination and Restraint*, Security Studies Center Proliferation Papers (2009).

[7] Kier Lieber and Daryl Press, "The New Era of Nuclear Weapons, Deterrence, and Conflict," *Strategic Studies Quarterly* 7, 1 (2013), 3-12.

[8] Scott Wilson, "Obama Proposes Scaling Back Nuclear Warheads," *Washington Post*, June 20 (2013).

[9] *Report on Nuclear Employment Strategy of the United States Specified in Section 491 of 10 U.S.C.* (2013), 6.

[10] For the concept of strategic stability see, Michael Gerson, "The Origins of Strategic Stability," in Elbridge Colby and Michael Gerson, editors, *Strategic Stability: Contending Interpretations*, U.S. Army War College Strategic Studies Institute (2013); Paul Bracken, "The Bomb Returns for a Second Act," Foreign Policy Research Institute E-Notes, November (2012).

[11] David Sanger, "Obama to Renew Drive for Cuts in Nuclear Arms," *New York Times*, February 10 (2013).

[12] Peter Baker and David Sanger, "Obama Has Plans to Cut U.S. Nuclear Arsenal, if Russia Reciprocates," *New York Times*, June 18 (2013).

[13] Personal communications between Dr. James Smith, Director of the United States Air Force Institute for National Security Studies, and strategic leaders at Headquarters United States Air Force.

[14] Manning, *Envisioning 2030*, 48.

[15] Robert Norris and Hans Kristensen, "Global Nuclear Stockpiles, 1945-2006," *Bulletin of the Atomic Scientists* 62, 4 (2006), 64-66.

[16] Estimated as of 18 December 2012 by the Federation of American Scientists. http://www.cnn.com/interactive/2013/03/world/nuclear-weapon-states/?hpt=hp_t1.

[17] *Nuclear Posture Review Report*, 43.

[18] Sanger, "Obama to Renew Drive for Cuts in Nuclear Arms."

[19] Baker and Sanger, "Obama Has Plans to Cut U.S. Nuclear Arsenal, if Russia Reciprocates."

[20] *New START Treaty Aggregate Numbers of Strategic Offensive Arms*, Bureau of Arms Control, Verification and Compliance, Fact Sheet, U.S. Department of State, July 1 (2013).

[21] Estimated as of 18 December 2012 by the Federation of American Scientists. http://www.cnn.com/interactive/2013/03/world/nuclear-weapon-states/?hpt=hp_t1.

[22] Bruce Blair, et al., "Smaller and Safer," *Foreign Affairs* 89, 5 (2010).

[23] John Deutch, "A Nuclear Posture for Today." *Foreign Affairs* 84, 1 (2005).

[24] James Forsyth, et al., "Remembrance of Things Past: The Enduring Value of Nuclear Weapons," *Strategic Studies Quarterly*, Spring (2010).

[25] Stephen Cimbala, "Matrix of Nonlinearity: Minimum Deterrence, Missile Defense, and Nuclear Arms Reduction," *Joint Force Quarterly* 62, 3 (2011).

[26] James Cartwright, et al., *Global Zero U.S. Nuclear Policy Commission Report: Modernizing U.S. Nuclear Strategy, Force Structure and Posture*, Global Zero (2012), 6.

[27] Dana Johnson, et al., "Triad, Dyad, Monad? Shaping the U.S. Force of the Future," *Mitchell Institute for Airpower Studies Report* 5 (2009).

[28] Adam Lowther, "Should the United States Maintain the Nuclear Triad?" *Air and Space Power Journal* 24, 2 (2010).

[29] Keir Lieber and Daryl Press, "Superiority Complex: Why America's Growing Nuclear Supremacy May Make War with China More Likely," *The Atlantic Monthly* 300, 1 (2007).

[30] Kier Lieber and Daryl Press, "The End of MAD? The Nuclear Dimension of U.S. Primacy," *International Security* 30, 4 (2006).

[31] Kier Lieber and Daryl Press, "The Nukes We Need," *Foreign Affairs* 88, 6 (2009).

[32] Kingston Reif, et al., "Pruning the Nuclear Triad? Pros and Cons of Bombers, Missiles, and Submarines," *Center for Arms Control and Non-Proliferation* 3 (2009).

[33] Jeffrey Larsen, et al., "Qualitative Considerations of Nuclear Forces at Lower Numbers and Implications for Future Arms Control Negotiations," *United States Air Force Institute for National Security Studies Occasional Paper* 68 (2012).

[34] For a thorough discussion of American grand strategy see John Zielinski, "What Price Sovereignty? The Two Faces of Engagement and the Paradox of Power: A Comparison of the Security and Grand Strategies of the United States and the European Union," *United States Air Force Institute for National Security Studies Strategic Papers Series* 3 (2012), 7-17.
http://www.usafa.edu/df/inss/Strategic%20Papers/2012/Zielinski%20What%20Price%20Sovereignty(26%20Nov%202012).pdf.

[35] *Geopolitics of the United States, Part 1: The Inevitable Empire* (2011).
http://www.stratfor.com/analysis/20110824-geopolitics-united-states-part-1-inevitable-empire.

[36] *Geopolitics of the United States, Part 2: American Identity and the Threats of Tomorrow* (2011).
http://www.stratfor.com/analysis/20110825-geopolitics-united-states-part-2-american-identity-threats-tomorrow.

[37] *National Security Strategy of the United States of America* (2010), 1-3, 7, 11-13.

[38] Ibid., 22.

[39] *Nuclear Posture Review Report*, 9.

[40] *Report on Nuclear Employment Strategy of the United States*, 2.

[41] *Nuclear Posture Review Report*, 11-12.

[42] Ibid., 15; *Report on Nuclear Employment Strategy of the United States*, 4.

[43] Manning, *Envisioning 2030*, 46.

[44] Estimated as of 18 December 2012 by the Federation of American Scientists.
http://www.cnn.com/interactive/2013/03/world/nuclear-weapon-states/?hpt=hp_t1.

[45] *New START Treaty Aggregate Numbers of Strategic Offensive Arms*.

[46] Ibid.

[47] *Nuclear Posture Review Report*, 15-16.

[48] *Report on Nuclear Employment Strategy of the United States*, 6.

[49] Ibid., 7.

[50] Baker and Sanger, "Obama Has Plans to Cut U.S. Nuclear Arsenal, if Russia Reciprocates."

[51] Ibid.

[52] Sanger, "Obama to Renew Drive for Cuts in Nuclear Arms."

[53] *Sustaining U.S. Global Leadership: Priorities for 21st Century Defense* (2012), 5.

[54] *Report on Nuclear Employment Strategy of the United States*, 8.

[55] George Friedman, *Britain's Strategy* (2012). http://www.stratfor.com/weekly/britains-strategy.

[56] Ibid.

[57] Ibid.

[58] *Securing Britain in an Age of Uncertainty: The Strategic Defense and Security Review* (2010), 9.

[59] Ibid., 11-12.

[60] Ibid., 18-19.

[61] Ibid., 37.

[62] Ibid.

[63] Ibid., 38-39.

[64] Estimated as of 18 December 2012 by the Federation of American Scientists. http://www.cnn.com/interactive/2013/03/world/nuclear-weapon-states/?hpt=hp_t1.

[65] *Geopolitics of France: Maintaining Its Influence in a Changing Europe* (2010). http://www.stratfor.com/analysis/geopolitics-france-maintaining-its-influence-changing-europe.

[66] Ibid.

[67] George Friedman, *France's Strategy* (2012). http://www.stratfor.com/weekly/frances-strategy.

[68] *The French White Paper on Defense and National Security* (2008), 14.

[69] See Zielinski, "What Price Sovereignty?," 8-9.

[70] *French White Paper on Defense and National Security*, 58.

[71] Ibid., 61.

[72] *Livre Blanc: Defense et Securite Nationale* (2013).

[73] Luis Simon, "The 2013 French Defense White Paper: Don't Write France Off Just Yet," *European Geostrategy Long Post* (2013), 3-4. http://www.europeangeostrategy.ideasoneurope.eu.

[74] *French White Paper on Defense and National Security*, 64-65.

[75] Ibid., 65.

[76] Estimated as of 18 December 2012 by the Federation of American Scientists. http://www.cnn.com/interactive/2013/03/world/nuclear-weapon-states/?hpt=hp_t1.

[77] *French White Paper on Defense and National Security*, 112-113.

[78] Ibid., 161-162 and 214-216.

[79] See Daniel Fiott, "The French Defense White Paper, 2013: the Global Balance-of-Power and European Defense Policy," *Ideas on Europe*, November 4 (2012). http://danielfiott.ideasoneurope.eu/2012/11/04/the-french-defence-white-paper-2013-the-global-balance-of-power-and-european-defence-policy/.

[80] Simon, "The 2013 French Defense White Paper," 1.

[81] *Active Engagement, Modern Defense: Strategic Concept for the Defense and Security of the Members of the North Atlantic Treaty Organization* (2010), 1.

[82] Ibid., 2-3.

[83] Ibid., 4-11.

[84] Ibid., 1-4, 7.

[85] Ibid.

[86] For a thorough discussion of European Union grand strategy see Zielinski, "What Price Sovereignty?," 18-25.

[87] Ibid., 24-25.

[88] Ibid., 25-27.

[89] *A Secure Europe in a Better World: European Security Strategy* (2003), 3.

[90] Ibid., 8-9.

[91] Ibid., 9-16.

[92] See Burkard Schmitt, editor, *Defense Procurement in the European Union: The Current Debate* (Paris: Institute for Security Studies, 2006); Jolyon Howorth, *Security and Defense Policy in the European Union* (New York: Palgrave MacMillan, 2007).

[93] See *Council Conclusions on Pooling and Sharing Military Capabilities* (Brussels: Council of the European Union, 2011).

[94] Thomas Valasek, "Surviving Austerity: The Case for a New Approach to European Union Military Cooperation," *Center for European Reform* (2011). http://www.cer.org.uk/pdf/rp_981.pdf.

[95] *European Defense Agency: Long-Term Vision* (2006). http://www.eda.europa.eu/genericite,.aspx?area=Organisation&id=146.

[96] See Seth Jones, *The Rise of European Security Cooperation* (Cambridge: Cambridge University Press, 2007).

[97] Catherine Field, "Britain and France to Work Together," *The New Zealand Herald*, November 4 (2010). http://www.nzherald.co.nz/world/news/article.cfm?c_id=2&objectid=10685127.

[98] *Treaty Between the United Kingdom and the French Republic for Defense and Security Cooperation* (2010). http://www.fco.gov.uk/resources/en/pdf/3706546/3892733/21824849/TrFrance1.2010DefenceSec.

[99] Ibid.

[100] Simon, "The 2013 French Defense White Paper," 1-5.

[101] See Jolyon Howorth, "Britain, France, and the European Union Defense Initiative," *Survival* 42 (2000).

[102] *Livre Blanc: Defense et Securite Nationale* (2013).

[103] "UK-French Defense Treaty," *BBC News*, November 2 (2010). http://www.bbc.co.uk/news/uk-politics-11672796.

[104] *Treaty Between the United Kingdom and the French Republic for Defense and Security Cooperation.*

[105] Des Browne, et al., *Building Mutual Security in the Euro-Atlantic Region*, Nuclear Threat Initiative (2013), 13.

[106] *Active Engagement, Modern Defense*, 1-4, 7; See also Walt Slocombe, *Nuclear Issues for NATO After the Strategic Concept* (Washington, DC: EUCOM Task Force, Atlantic Council of the United States, 2011); David Yost, *Adapting NATO's Deterrence Posture: The Alliance's New Strategic Concept and Implication for Nuclear Policy, Non-Proliferation, Arms Control, and Disarmament: A Report on a Workshop in Tallinn, 4-6 May 2011* (Rome: NATO Defense College, 2011).

[107] Hans Kristensen, *U.S. Nuclear Weapons in Europe: A Review of Post-Cold War Policy, Force Levels, and War Planning* (New York: Natural Resources Defense Council, 2005).

[108] *NATO Revises Nuclear Policy* (2010). http://www.armscontrol.org/print/4590.

[109] See *The Nuclear Planning Group*. http://www.nato.int/cps/en/natolive/topics_50069.htm.

[110] *NATO Revises Nuclear Policy* (2010).

[111] See David Yost, *The U.S. and Nuclear Deterrence in Europe* (London: Oxford University Press for the International Institute for Strategic Studies, 1999).

[112] See Sam Nunn, "NATO Nuclear Policy and Euro-Atlantic Security," *Survival* 52, 2 (2010); James Schlesinger, Chairman, *Report of the Secretary of Defense Task Force on DoD Nuclear Weapons Management, Phase II: Review of the DoD Nuclear Mission* (Arlington: Secretary of Defense Task Force on DoD Nuclear Weapons Management, 2008); William Perry, *America's Strategic Posture: The Final Report of the Congressional Commission on the Strategic Posture of the United States* (Washington, DC: United States Institute of Peace Press, 2009).

[113] Leo Michel, "Construct a U.S.-U.K.-French 'Entente Cordiale'," *Defense News* (2013). http://www.defensenews.com/article/20130407/DEFFEAT05/304070010/Construct-U-S-U-K-French-8216-Entente-Cordiale-8217-.

[114] For alternative approaches to deterrence see David Yost, "New Approaches to Deterrence in Britain, France, and the United States," *International Affairs* 81 (2005).

[115] Oliver Thranert, "U.S. Nuclear Forces in Europe to Zero? Yes, but Not Yet," *Proliferation Analysis* (2008).

[116] Craig Cohen, "European Trilateral Track 2 Nuclear Dialogue," *Center for Strategic and International Studies* (2013).

[117] Ibid.

[118] Ibid.

[119] *Global Zero U.S. Nuclear Policy Commission Report*, 7.

[120] Reif, et al., "Pruning the Nuclear Triad?"

[121] Lowther, "Should the United States Maintain the Nuclear Triad?"

[122] Stephanie Spies and John Warden, *Forging a Consensus for a Sustainable U.S. Nuclear Posture: A Report of the CSIS Nuclear Consensus Working Group* (New York: Rowman and Littlefield, 2013).

[123] Ibid., VI-VII.

[124] Barry Blechman, "A Sustainable U.S. Nuclear Posture," in *Forging a Consensus for a Sustainable U.S. Nuclear Posture: A Report of the CSIS Nuclear Consensus Working Group* (New York: Rowman and Littlefield, 2013), 16.

[125] Linton Brooks, "The Elements of a Possible Political Agreement to Maintain a Safe, Secure, Reliable, and Effective Nuclear Deterrent," in *Forging a Consensus for a Sustainable U.S. Nuclear Posture: A Report of the CSIS Nuclear Consensus Working Group* (New York: Rowman and Littlefield, 2013), 21.

[126] Robert DeGrasse, "Proposed Nuclear Posture and Sustainable Strategy," in *Forging a Consensus for a Sustainable U.S. Nuclear Posture: A Report of the CSIS Nuclear Consensus Working Group* (New York: Rowman and Littlefield, 2013), 27.

[127] Robert Joseph, "Forging Consensus for a Sustainable U.S. Nuclear Posture," in *Forging a Consensus for a Sustainable U.S. Nuclear Posture: A Report of the CSIS Nuclear Consensus Working Group* (New York: Rowman and Littlefield, 2013), 33.

[128] Frank Klotz, "Achieving Consensus for a Sustainable U.S. Nuclear Posture," in *Forging a Consensus for a Sustainable U.S. Nuclear Posture: A Report of the CSIS Nuclear Consensus Working Group* (New York: Rowman and Littlefield, 2013), 36-37.

[129] George Perkovich, "Achieving Consensus for a Sustainable U.S. Nuclear Posture," in *Forging a Consensus for a Sustainable U.S. Nuclear Posture: A Report of the CSIS Nuclear Consensus Working Group* (New York: Rowman and Littlefield, 2013), 46.

[130] Alyson Bailes, "Differentiated Risk and Threat Perceptions of European Union Members and Their Impact on European Security Cooperation," *Foreign Policy* 29 (2004) 3-4.

[131] Marko Papic, *North Atlantic Treaty Organization's Lack of a Strategic Concept* (2010). http://www.stratfor.com/weekly/20101001_NATO_lack_strategic_concept.

[132] Franklin Miller, "NATO's Nuclear Future: Self-Centered Policies Threaten Collective Security," Remarks at the Brookings Institution, July 19 (2011). http://www.acus.org/natosource/nato's-nuclear-future-sel-centered-policies-threaten-collective-security.

[133] *French White Paper on Defense and National Security*, 65.

[134] "Trilateral Nuclear Dialogues: Toward a Common P3 Approach on Nuclear Non-Proliferation, Energy Use, Disarmament and Material Security," *Center for Strategic and International Studies* (2009). http://www.csis.org/files/publication/091120_csis_trilateral_nuclear_dialogues_statement.pdf; "The Roles and Salience of U.S., British and French Nuclear Weapons," *Center for Strategic and International Studies* (2010), http://www.csis.org/files/publication/100706_Role_P3_Nuclear_Weapons-FINAL-signed.pdf; "Role of Nuclear Weapons in NATO Security," *Center for Strategic and International Studies* (2010), http://www.csis.org/files/publication/101019_Role_NW_NATO.pdf; "CSIS European Trilateral Track 2 Nuclear Dialogues Statement: Toward an Appropriate Mix of Conventional, Nuclear, and Missile Defense Forces," *Center for Strategic and International Studies* (2011), http://www.csis.org/files/publication/110824_European_Trilat_Appropriate_Mix_Statement.pdf.

REFERENCES

Active Engagement, Modern Defense: Strategic Concept for the Defense and Security of the Members of the North Atlantic Treaty Organization. 2010.

Bailes, A. "Differentiated Risk and Threat Perceptions of European Union Members and Their Impact on European Security Cooperation." *Foreign Policy* 29, 3-4. 2004.

Baker, P. and D. Sanger. "Obama Has Plans to Cut U.S. Nuclear Arsenal, if Russia Reciprocates." *New York Times.* June 18, 2013.

Blair, B., et al. "Smaller and Safer." *Foreign Affairs* 89, 5. 2010.

Blechman, B. "A Sustainable U.S. Nuclear Posture," in S. Spies and J. Warden, *Forging a Consensus for a Sustainable U.S. Nuclear Posture: A Report of the CSIS Nuclear Consensus Working Group.* New York: Rowman and Littlefield. 2013.

Bracken, P. "The Bomb Returns for a Second Act." Foreign Policy Research Institute E-Notes. November, 2012.

Bracken, P. *The Second Nuclear Age: Strategy, Danger, and the New Power Politics.* New York: Times Books. 2012.

Brooks, L. "The Elements of a Possible Political Agreement to Maintain a Safe, Secure, Reliable, and Effective Nuclear Deterrent," in S. Spies and J. Warden, *Forging a Consensus for a Sustainable U.S. Nuclear Posture: A Report of the CSIS Nuclear Consensus Working Group.* New York: Rowman and Littlefield. 2013.

Browne, D., et al. *Building Mutual Security in the Euro-Atlantic Region.* Nuclear Threat Initiative. 2013.

Cartwright, J., et al. *Global Zero U.S. Nuclear Policy Commission Report: Modernizing U.S. Nuclear Strategy, Force Structure and Posture.* Global Zero. 2012.

Cimbala, S. "Matrix of Nonlinearity: Minimum Deterrence, Missile Defense, and Nuclear Arms Reduction." *Joint Force Quarterly* 62, 3. 2011.

Cohen, C. "European Trilateral Track 2 Nuclear Dialogue." *Center for Strategic and International Studies.* 2013.

Colby, E. and M. Gerson, editors. *Strategic Stability: Contending Interpretations.* U.S. Army War College Strategic Studies Institute. 2013.

Council Conclusions on Pooling and Sharing Military Capabilities. Brussels: Council of the European Union. 2011.

"CSIS European Trilateral Track 2 Nuclear Dialogues Statement: Toward an Appropriate Mix of Conventional, Nuclear, and Missile Defense Forces." *Center for Strategic and International Studies.* 2011.

DeGrasse, R. "Proposed Nuclear Posture and Sustainable Strategy," in S. Spies and J. Warden, *Forging a Consensus for a Sustainable U.S. Nuclear Posture: A Report of the CSIS Nuclear Consensus Working Group.* New York: Rowman and Littlefield. 2013.

Deutch, J. "A Nuclear Posture for Today." *Foreign Affairs* 84, 1. 2005.

European Defense Agency: Long-Term Vision. 2006.

Evans, G. and Y. Kawaguchi. *Eliminating Nuclear Threats: A Practical Guide for Global Policymakers – Report of the International Commission on Nuclear Non-Proliferation and Disarmament.* Canberra: Paragon. 2009.

Field, C. "Britain and France to Work Together." *The New Zealand Herald.* November 4, 2010.

Fiott, D. "The French Defense White Paper, 2013: The Global Balance-of-Power and European Defense Policy." *Ideas on Europe.* November 4, 2012.

Forsyth, J., B. Saltzman, and G. Schaub. "Remembrance of Things Past: The Enduring Value of Nuclear Weapons." *Strategic Studies Quarterly.* Spring, 2010.

French White Paper on Defense and National Security. 2008

Friedman, G. *Britain's Strategy*. 2012.

Friedman, G. *France's Strategy*. 2012.

Geopolitics of France: Maintaining Its Influence in a Changing Europe. 2010.

Geopolitics of the United States, Part 1: The Inevitable Empire. 2011.

Geopolitics of the United States, Part 2: American Identity and the Threats of Tomorrow. 2011.

Gerson, M. "The Origins of Strategic Stability," in E. Colby and M. Gerson, editors, *Strategic Stability: Contending Interpretations*. U.S. Army War College Strategic Studies Institute. 2013.

Gottemoeller, R. "New Strategic Arms Reduction Treaty: Security Through 21st-Century Verification." *Arms Control Today*. 2010.

Howorth, J. "Britain, France, and the European Union Defense Initiative." *Survival* 42. 2000.

Howorth, J. *Security and Defense Policy in the European Union*. New York: Palgrave MacMillan. 2007.

Johnson, D., C. Bowie, and R. Haffa. "Triad, Dyad, Monad? Shaping the U.S. Force of the Future." *Mitchell Institute for Airpower Studies Report* 5. 2009.

Jones, S. *The Rise of European Security Cooperation*. Cambridge: Cambridge University Press. 2007.

Joseph, R. "Forging Consensus for a Sustainable U.S. Nuclear Posture," in S. Spies and J. Warden, *Forging a Consensus for a Sustainable U.S. Nuclear Posture: A Report of the CSIS Nuclear Consensus Working Group*. New York: Rowman and Littlefield. 2013.

Klotz, F. "Achieving Consensus for a Sustainable U.S. Nuclear Posture," in S. Spies and J. Warden, *Forging a Consensus for a Sustainable U.S. Nuclear Posture: A Report of the CSIS Nuclear Consensus Working Group*. New York: Rowman and Littlefield. 2013.

Kristensen, H. *U.S. Nuclear Weapons in Europe: A Review of Post-Cold War Policy, Force Levels, and War Planning*. New York: Natural Resources Defense Council. 2005.

Larsen, J., et al. "Qualitative Considerations of Nuclear Forces at Lower Numbers and Implications for Future Arms Control Negotiations." *United States Air Force Institute for National Security Studies Occasional Paper* 68. 2012.

Lieber, K. and D. Press. "The End of MAD? The Nuclear Dimension of U.S. Primacy." *International Security* 30, 4. 2006.

Lieber, K. and D. Press. "The New Era of Nuclear Weapons, Deterrence, and Conflict." *Strategic Studies Quarterly* 7, 1. 2013.

Lieber, K. and D. Press. "The Nukes We Need." *Foreign Affairs* 88, 6. 2009.

Lieber, K. and D. Press. "Superiority Complex: Why America's Growing Nuclear Supremacy May Make War with China More Likely." *The Atlantic Monthly* 300, 1. 2007.

Livre Blanc: Defense et Securite Nationale. 2013.

Lowther, A. "Should the United States Maintain the Nuclear Triad?" *Air and Space Power Journal* 24, 2. 2010.

Manning, R. *Envisioning 2030: U.S. Strategy for a Post-Western World*. Atlantic Council. 2013.

Michel, L. "Construct a U.S.-U.K.-French 'Entente Cordiale'." *Defense News*. 2013.

Miller, F. "NATO's Nuclear Future: Self-Centered Policies Threaten Collective Security." Remarks at the Brookings Institution on July 19, 2011.

National Security Strategy of the United States of America. 2010.

NATO Revises Nuclear Policy. 2010.

New START Treaty Aggregate Numbers of Strategic Offensive Arms. Bureau of Arms Control, Verification and Compliance, Fact Sheet, U.S. Department of State. July 1, 2013.

Norris, R. and H. Kristensen. "Global Nuclear Stockpiles, 1945-2006." *Bulletin of the Atomic Scientists* 62, 4. 2006.

Nuclear Planning Group.

Nuclear Posture Review Report. 2010.

Nuclear Weapons: Who Has What? 2013.

Nunn, S. "NATO Nuclear Policy and Euro-Atlantic Security." *Survival* 52, 2. 2010.

Papic, M. *NATO's Lack of a Strategic Concept.* 2010.

Perkovich, G. "Achieving Consensus for a Sustainable U.S. Nuclear Posture," in S. Spies and J. Warden, *Forging a Consensus for a Sustainable U.S. Nuclear Posture: A Report of the CSIS Nuclear Consensus Working Group.* New York: Rowman and Littlefield. 2013.

Perry, W. *America's Strategic Posture: The Final Report of the Congressional Commission on the Strategic Posture of the United States.* Washington, DC: United States Institute of Peace Press. 2009.

Reif, K., T. Sharp, and K. Bansak. "Pruning the Nuclear Triad? Pros and Cons of Bombers, Missiles, and Submarines." *Center for Arms Control and Non-Proliferation* 3. 2009.

Report on Nuclear Employment Strategy of the United States Specified in Section 491 of 10 U.S.C. 2013.

"Role of Nuclear Weapons in NATO Security." *Center for Strategic and International Studies.* 2010.

"The Roles and Salience of U.S., British and French Nuclear Weapons." *Center for Strategic and International Studies.* 2010.

Sanger, D. "Obama to Renew Drive for Cuts in Nuclear Arms." *New York Times.* February 10, 2013.

Schlesinger, J., Chairman. *Report of the Secretary of Defense Task Force on DoD Nuclear Weapons Management, Phase II: Review of the DoD Nuclear Mission.* Arlington: Secretary of Defense Task Force on DoD Nuclear Weapons Management. 2008.

Schmitt, B., editor. *Defense Procurement in the European Union: The Current Debate.* Paris: Institute for Security Studies. 2006.

Secure Europe in a Better World: European Security Strategy. 2003.

Securing Britain in an Age of Uncertainty: The Strategic Defense and Security Review. 2010.

Simon, L. "The 2013 French Defense White Paper: Don't Write France Off Just Yet." *European Geostrategy Long Post.* 2013.

Slocombe, W. *Nuclear Issues for NATO After the Strategic Concept.* Washington, DC: EUCOM Task Force, Atlantic Council of the United States. 2011.

Spies, S. and J. Warden. *Forging a Consensus for a Sustainable U.S. Nuclear Posture: A Report of the CSIS Nuclear Consensus Working Group.* New York: Rowman and Littlefield. 2013.

Sustaining U.S. Global Leadership: Priorities for 21st Century Defense. 2012.

Thranert, O. "U.S. Nuclear Forces in Europe to Zero? Yes, but Not Yet." *Proliferation Analysis.* 2008.

Treaty Between the United Kingdom and the French Republic for Defense and Security Cooperation. 2010.

"Trilateral Nuclear Dialogues: Toward a Common P3 Approach on Nuclear Non-Proliferation, Energy Use, Disarmament and Material Security." *Center for Strategic and International Studies.* 2009.

"UK-French Defense Treaty." *BBC News.* November 2, 2010.

Valasek, T. "Surviving Austerity: The Case for a New Approach to European Union Military Cooperation." *Center for European Reform.* 2011.

Walker, W. *President-Elect Obama and Nuclear Disarmament: Between Elimination and Restraint.* Security Studies Center Proliferation Papers. 2009.

Wilson, S. "Obama Proposes Scaling Back Nuclear Warheads." *Washington Post*. June 20, 2013.

Yost, D. *Adapting NATO's Deterrence Posture: The Alliance's New Strategic Concept and Implication for Nuclear Policy, Non-Proliferation, Arms Control, and Disarmament: A Report on a Workshop in Tallinn, 4-6 May 2011.* Rome: NATO Defense College. 2011.

Yost, D. "New Approaches to Deterrence in Britain, France, and the United States." *International Affairs* 81. 2005.

Yost, D. *The U.S. and Nuclear Deterrence in Europe*. London: Oxford University Press for the International Institute for Strategic Studies. 1999.

Zielinski, J. "What Price Sovereignty? The Two Faces of Engagement and the Paradox of Power: A Comparison of the Security and Grand Strategies of the United States and the European Union." *United States Air Force Institute for National Security Studies Strategic Papers Series* 3. 2012.

www.ingramcontent.com/pod-product-compliance
Lightning Source LLC
Chambersburg PA
CBHW080634290526
45790CB00007B/3066

9 781502 923851